Word Up:

Little Languaging Hacks for Big Change

by Dani Katz

Word Up: Little Languaging Hacks for Big Change

By Dani Katz

ISBN-13: 978-1979154192
ISBN-10: 1979154198

Acknowledgments

Big ups, and oodles of gratitude to R. Neville Johnston for getting shot point blank in the chest, and dying, and bringing back this extraordinary languaging perspective, and initiating me into its magic.

Justin Frank Polgar: a zillion iterations of infinite, heart-drenched gratitude for our Conscious Awesome word wizardry. Thank you for being an ever-present sounding board throughout the writing of this book, and – well, al(l)ways.

Thank you to my rebel-rebel Aquarian sister, Hilary Bromberg, for the encouragement, the read-through, the support and the superfoods.

Oodles of high-kicking, shimmy-shimmying gratitude to Zoë Segal for the super, very upleveled title.

Thank you, Cory Goldberg, for availing yourself to another book edit; and for carving out the time to put so much loving, focused, brilliant and precise attention on every single word; and for – yet again - making my work better.

Contents

Preface

As a writer (journalist, essayist, screenwriter, copywriter, cartoonist and all-around word nerd), I spend the vast majority of my time engaging words – channeling, weaving, wrestling, massaging, arranging, rearranging, pondering, deconstructing, poking at, playing with – you get the gist, yes? I've been known to spend upwards of forty-five minutes at a time reworking a single sentence, delighting in the process of nudging words into different structures and relationships, delving deeper, and deeper still, into their meanings, their associations and their functionality, all in service to the most precise translation possible.

Years ago, a sweeping batch of synchronicities introduced me to the vibrational frequencies of words. My mind was blown wide open, and I immersed myself in the study and application of esoteric languaging systems. The works of David Bohm, Richard Rudd, Noam Chomsky, Terence McKenna, Neville Goddard, Buckminster Fuller, J. Krishnamurti, R. Neville Johnston, G. I. Gurdjieff, et al activated an entirely new languaging paradigm that radically transformed my relationship to my Self, as well as the world at large, in countless and extraordinary ways.

As I integrated my nascent understanding of language as reality creation technology, all these words I spent my days weaving began to reveal a dazzling array of codes that shape every aspect of our experience. I started attuning to languaging patterns in such a way that I could instantly see where folks were getting in their own way by simply tracking their word choices. Emboldened by this insight, I turned my attention inward; tuning into my own communication habits from this newly expanded perspective, and began deconstructing the blocks, patterns and belief systems unconsciously informing my communication habits. It was as though I'd removed a hazy filter that had been shrouding my awareness. I finally understood – née grokked[1] – how we really, truly are 100% responsible for our experience of reality, and how our every word functions to create this experience, and this reality.

Most wonderful to report is that my relationships – to others, as well as to my Self - continue to deepen and flourish as a direct result of my consistent utilization of these tools I have come to refer to as Quantum Languaging. As I continue to hone my ear, and attune my awareness to the vibratory coherence of the words I use, I realize with increasing certainty that my languaging patterns hold the keys to my awakening; and that every block, shadow and limitation that is mine to transmute is revealed in my personal lexicon, in the words I habitually use to create

---

1   **grok**; v. to understand profoundly and intuitively

my Self, and the world at large. And so it is that when I get lost in the shadows, and the craggy unkempt corners of my mind; and I doubt, and contract and freak way out; it is these Quantum Languaging hacks that bring me back to center, and to the Truth of my omniscopic light.

om · ni · sco · pic; *adj.*
every moment access to every potentiality that is, was or will be. [2]

---

2   Language, like culture, is an ever-unfolding work in progress. When we happen upon a gaping hole in our lexicon, it is our responsibility to toss some linguistic novelty into our collective mix. To this end, I give us this handy-dandy new word. Yay for quantum lexicon expansion!

I am what I say I am. I am the words I ascribe to my Self. And just as there are infinite insidious ways for me to use language to disempower myself and others, there are just as many opportunities for me to consciously employ words to lift us up, and to shape our world for the (even more) wonderful. As such, I am offering these Quantum Languaging hacks to those of us poised at the forefront of this extraordinary paradigm shift we Earthlings are currently navigating; to the peaceful (r)evolutionaries who – armed with open hearts, expanded perspectives and the integrated understanding of our inherent Oneness – are cocreating our world for the (even more) wonderful, in service to the greatest good of all.

Introduction

As challenging as it may be to grok, time is indeed speeding up. Gone are the days when friends and associates eagerly engage our go-nowhere ramblings, patiently trusting that we have a point, and that it's not quite as disjointed or tangential as it sounds. Our ever-quickening Technological Age usually graces us with a paradoxically-shrinking minute or two of people's attention in which to make an impact, and be heard. Tweets, log lines, status updates and elevator pitches – these hyper-limited, über-truncated platforms are shaping our capacity to focus, and receive information, drastically shrinking the time we can reasonably allot to our ideas' transmission. As such, it makes sense to choose our words carefully and consciously, while making deft use of languaging hacks that allow our messages to land as quickly, effectively and efficiently as possible.

If we can really understand the problem, the answer will come out of it, because the answer is not separate from the problem.

— **Jiddu Krishnamurti**

At the same time, we – a singular species of Earthlings - are facing a spectacular array of global challenges, which are inviting the swift execution of innovative restructuring solutions that will allow us to rebalance our planet, such that we can coexist in peace, unity and abundance, as a healthy, thriving all of us. And while this isn't to inspire even an inkling of fear (because we live in a reality forged of equal and opposite forces, which means our every challenge necessarily contains its corresponding solution), it is to say that evolutionary circumstances are converging to nudge us out of our languid slumber. We have lost the privilege of lolly-gagging languaging that allows us to dilly-dally in perpetual procrastination mode. It is time for us to galvanize a singular collective intention to steer our spaceship Earth onto a more functional, inclusive, sustainable trajectory, immediately.

> *Our ability to destroy ourselves is the mirror image of our ability to save ourselves, and what is lacking is the clear vision of what should be done...What needs to be done is that fundamental, ontological conceptions of reality need to be redone. We need a new language, and to have a new language we must have a new reality...A new reality will generate a new language, a new language will fix a new reality, and make it part of this reality.*
>
> **– Terence McKenna**

As we shift from an old paradigm (*old p.*) of scarcity, limitation, competition and divisiveness to a new paradigm (*new p.*) of unity, sustainability, abundance and cooperation, we are necessarily relinquishing a language steeped in fear, separation and limitation, instead choosing to utilize a language of inclusion, confidence, abundance and empowerment. While the former tethers us to an outdated perspective that would have us believe we are but a chaotic assortment of separate, disempowered beings doomed to fight over a limited array of finite resources in a third dimension enslaved by linear time, Quantum Languaging marks a new communication paradigm wherein we lay claim to the truth of our sovereignty, as well as our omniscopic potential, emboldened by the knowledge that our every word has the power to support us in gracefully transitioning to a present moment reality marked by health, peace, prosperity and happiness for all beings, now.

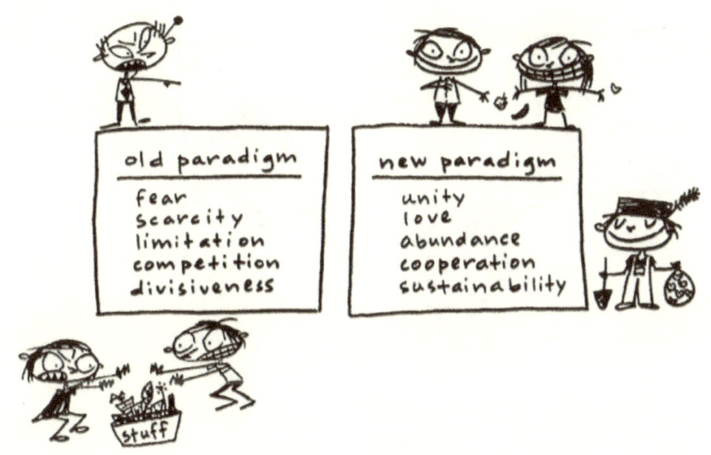

The revolution will be complete when the language is perfect.

– George Orwell

The truth is, most of our languaging choices aren't actually choices at all. They are habits. These habits shape our reality. To this end, we are wise to develop languaging habits that are aligned with the reality we'd most like to experience.

This book comprises a consciously curated collection of languaging hacks gleaned from exhaustive research, decades of experience and a handful of mystical downloads. In compiling these Quantum Languaging tools, tricks and tenets, I am not reinventing any wheels. I am, however, absolutely reframing our world, as well as our relationship to it, for the infinitely more creative, collaborative and empowered.

I invite us to use these languaging hacks as tools to shake up the habituated, old p. thought patterns, belief systems and languaging strategies that have historically kept us tethered to a shortsighted paradigm we've outgrown, and to attune us to the vibrational frequencies of this stunning new p. we, the peaceful (r)evolutionaries, are together stewarding. In addition to being radically effective, and thoroughly transformative, they're super, very fun. I promise.

xodk

The syntactical nature of reality, the real secret of magic, is that the world is made of words. And if you know the words that the world is made of, you can make of it whatever you wish.

— Terence McKenna

Part 1

The Fundamentals

Words: The Great and Mighty Multitaskers

The limits of my language mean the limits of my world.

– Ludwig Wittgenstein

Is-*ness Establishers*

Words do many things, on lots of levels at once. Words help us exchange information and cultivate relationships. They allow us to think, create, express and figure stuff out. But, before they perform any of these awesome functions, words do something even more profound: they establish existential validity.

Everything we know to exist has a word that represents it. It's how we know something exists: it's a word. In acting as symbolic reference points, words render things so, thus allowing every single thing that is, has been or will ever be to claim/sustain its existence.

Creation Technology

Words are the vehicles upon which our thoughts, ideas and inventions ride - from the invisible realms of inspiration, to the dense world of third dimensional form. First comes the idea, which exists as nebulous mystery fluff in our minds. We then use words to translate this nebulous mystery fluff into 3D structure. Whether we write them down, speak them aloud or silently employ them while constructing visionary notions within the confines of our minds, words are the tools that allow us to manifest our ideas in the material realm.

The success of this materialization process is inextricably bound to the words we use to communicate our ideas: the more precise the communication, the more integrous[3] the idea's realization.

Thought-Shapers

The structure of language determines not only thought, but reality itself.

— Noam Chomsky

---

3   **integrous**; *adj.* the state of having, or being characterized by integrity. Also, while we're on the subject, doesn't it strike you as odd that - officially, at least - the English language has no adjectival version of the word *integrity*? Contemplation fodder...

Language is an organized collection of words used by a specified group of beings to communicate. Language structures thought. Also, the whole world. Everything we experience is filtered through our senses, and then organized in our brains by way of syntactical orientation, which is structured through language. Language shapes the way our brains actually function, thus providing the context for our every shred of experience.

Cultural-Contextualizer

Culture is a manmade overlay we use to organize reality. It comprises our lore, our activities, our etiquette, our institutions, our currency and our media. Language is the filter through which the aspects of a culture are formed and sustained.

> *Language is power, life and the instrument of culture, the instrument of domination and liberation.*
>
> *-* **Angela Carter**

Take French, or Spanish, or any of the European languages that structure their grammar such that they say: I *have hunger, or I have 57 years;* while in English, we say: I *am hungry, or I am 57 years old.*

This seemingly minor syntactical difference has an enormous influence on how we identify ourselves in relation to our experiences, as well as to our years incarnate. The European language structure creates distance between the subject and the action, positioning she who hungers, or he who has celebrated fifty-seven birthdays as witnesses to the events they experience. Conversely, English grammar inextricably links us to our experiences such that we – by syntactical default – verily merge with our belly rumbles and our sun spins. This ostensibly insignificant grammatical differential has a rather massive effect on the cultures at large, and the psyches of the beings that comprise them, with Europeans holding their ideas, their identities and their experiences far more loosely than Americans, who are so identified with their ideas that they feel the need to arm themselves with a surplus of firearms and long-range ex-plosives to defend them; to say nothing of our national obsession with youth, and our contentious relationship with the aging process, which have together spawned a billion dollar "anti-aging" industry whose very languaging only serves to keep us at combative odds with time's supposedly linear progression while fostering a debilitating collective neuroses about sunspots and crow's feet.

> *Language is not merely a means of expression and communication; it is an instrument of experiencing, thinking and feeling. Our ideas and experiences are not independent of language; they are all integral parts of the same pattern, the warp and woof of the same texture.*
>
> **- William Chomsky**

To this end, language isn't merely a tool that allows us to describe our experience of reality; rather, it is a filter that shapes said reality itself at a fundamental level. This phenomenon is but one of the many nifty and mind-bending aspects of living in a relative third dimensional construct wherein the very act of observing reality shapes it, because there is no singular objective reality – at least, not on this planet, there isn't. Reality is a co-creative collaboration between subject and object; and language is our primary means of sculpting it.

The Subconscious Mind. *Whoa.*

The subconscious mind comprises our habits, beliefs, emotions, preferences, conditioning and imagination. It is programmed through words, and repetition; and, it is responsible for 95% of our decisions and behavior.

Ninety-five fucking percent.

The subconscious mind is very, very different from the conscious mind. For starters, it's thoroughly illogical. The subconscious mind doesn't understand past and future. It interprets all input in the present moment. Also, it's literal, which means it doesn't understand nuance, or sarcasm, or metaphor. This can get super, very dicey when, exhausted from a long, uphill sprint towards our daily destiny, we mutter *I need a break*, which the subconscious is poised to interpret as a direct command.

Hiya, fractured femur!

Did I mention that the subconscious mind is what connects us to universal intelligence, and thus directs space/time to configure according to its interpretations of our commands, filtered through its own unique programming?

As if these aspects weren't tricky enough, the subconscious mind doesn't process negatives. This means that when we say: *I am not afraid*, the subconscious connects to the directive/vibration of fear (instead of the implied, though unarticulated *courage* we are actually intending), and goes about taking the fear reference as an order, and then organizes reality, and our nervous systems, accordingly.

Oy.

Given that words are our A-number-one means of programming these otherwise irrational subsoncsciouses of ours, we are wise to remember this fundamental Quantum Languaging axiom: Every word matters.

Everything is Vibration.

If you want to find the secrets of the universe, think in terms of energy, frequency and vibration.

- Nikola Tesla

Everything in our known reality - when broken down to its smallest, most fundamental material unit - is vibration. Words included. Every word vibrates at its own unique frequency. These frequencies do far more than transmit definitions to our brains. They broadcast hyper-nuanced codes and signals to our emotional bodies, our energetic bodies and our psyches - as well as to the universe at large. Because, despite all reductive left-brained, patriarchal paradigms to the contrary, we humans aren't just meat-suit encased monkey minds driven by intellect and that good ol' biological imperative. Rather, we are multidimensional beings – as abstract, intuitive and emotional as we are linear, rational and logical – sending and receiving various levels and layers of information that speak to all of our complex aspects with our every word.

Quantum Languaging organizes our communication patterns with all of these aspects in mind, streamlining our ideas by way of integrated languaging hacks that harmonize these various dimensions in service to the greatest possible good of all.

Quantum, *Huh?*

This brings us to how Quantum Languaging got its nifty name. *Quantum* is a derivation of the Latin word quantus, which means: *How much? How far? To what extent?* For our intents and purposes, *quantum* points rather perfectly to the communication paradigm we are together exploring, in that it implies the whole proverbial shebang - encompassing all the multidimensional implications our each and every word conjures. Quantum Languaging invites us to consider our languaging choices far beyond mere intellectual connotation, or dictionary definition, to include the energetic frequencies encoded in our words, as well as the functions those energies perform, and the effects they have on us, and the world at large.

Contraction, Expansion, Neutrality, Oh My!

According to the universal laws of physics, every shred of our material reality is comprised of particles that exist in a state of constant flux between expansion and contraction. Words function the same way, with some vibrating at frequencies that expand, others vibrating at frequencies that contract, and plenty that simply vibrate at the frequency of neutrality.

Quantum Languaging Somatics:

Give yourself a few minutes to sit quietly in a comfortable space. Dial down the volume of your thoughts, while paying attention to your breath, and to the grounded, centered, wholeness that you are. Say the following words aloud, one a time, noticing the feelings that accompany each one. Let go of connotative associations, and focus instead on the physical experience of each word – how each one feels in your throat, and in your belly, and in your heart, and in your pinky toe. Note any colors, images, emotions, associations or temperature shifts the utterings inspire.

yes

red

now

alone

oatmeal

deadline

horizon

fence

kitten

traffic

forest

tomorrow

turquoise

Note that there are no wrong answers here. We are simply familiarizing ourselves with a different dimensional experience of language.

Expansive Communication is Efficient Communication

Expansive words are supportive allies that do the heavy lifting for us. Expansive words open up our audience to receive, thus rendering folks more available to hear, grok and embrace our messages.

Words like *no, can't, should, hate* and *don't* not only reflect our own blocks and limiting beliefs, they inspire contraction in the folks we are addressing, which pretty much defeats the purpose of communication, which is to say: Let's give those contracting words a rest, shall we?

Efficient Communication is Effective Communication

It's easier to toss a ball through a gaping hole than a tiny slit.[4]

— Dani Katz

---

4   Despite the snickers this statement inevitably illicits in every Quantum Languaging workshop I've (yet) taught, it is neither pervy metaphor, nor crotch reference.

While we are indeed vast and powerful omniscopic beings, realizing our human potential while evolving our culture/world for the better invites us to intelligently meter out finite amounts of daily energy allotments. Rock climbers are guided by this knowledge; training long and hard to make the fewest possible moves while scaling as much rock face as they can. This strategy maximizes productivity while minimizing energetic output, thus ensuring that climbers have enough stamina to summit massive peaks.

Energetically efficient communication works similarly, inviting us to be clear, direct, precise and concise, while guiding us to be mindful of our words' intellectual connotations and vibratory resonance, as well as their ability to create and sustain expansive space within the field of communication. Maximally effective communication not only allows for precise translation of abstract conceptual mind stuff, it saves time and conserves energy, which we can then apply to other areas of our life, like studying Portuguese, decalcifying our pineal glands and mastering the G to F chord transition on our sustainably-sourced ukuleles.

Part 2

Words To Avoid

try

Whether it was watching Yoda on the big screen, or being balled out by our seventh grade softball coach, at some point or another, we've all heard a variation of the *Don't try; do* schpiel. Still, that insidious little cop-out of a verb continues to infiltrate our lexicon, inadvertently holding us back, slowing us down and cramping our style.

> *Do or do not. There is no try.*
>
> *- Yoda*

No other being on the planet *tries*, save humans. Grass doesn't try to grow. Bees don't try to fly. They grow, and they fly, and they don't run any neurotic headtrips in the interim, attempting to rewrite their nascent foibles, misfires or fuck-ups to appease the butt-hurt egos they don't even have, because they don't doubt their dharma.

dhar • ma, *n.*
an individual's lifetime duty, as relates to her destiny; the pursuit and execution of one's nature and true calling in the context of their individual role in the collective cosmic dance.

The problem with *try* – well-intended though it may be – is that *try* vibrates at the frequency of doubt, thus introducing the possibility of failure into the scenario in question. It would be one thing if *try* could insinuate itself into a conversation while quietly keeping its self-esteem issues to itself; but, that's not how language works. Every word we utter doubles as a direct command to the universe wherein it attracts like-vibrating experiences and circumstances to the speaker. *Try* broadcasts doubt far and wide, while carving deep doubt grooves into the brain, and the subconscious, verily daring the universe to bestow failure upon every act it modifies, while inadvertently attracting doubty/faily experiences to itself.

When we claim our actions with confidence, while eschewing the urge to mitigate them with "try," our paths to success are free and clear. Weighed down by the concept of *trying*, as well as all the doubt and failure frequencies the word activates, suddenly these concepts are given unconscious credence, and become possibilities we entertain, which significantly increases the likelihood of their manifestation.

As if that weren't enough of a bummer, doubt is contagious, which means that when we use the word *try*, we activate the doubt frequency in the folks we are addressing; thus, spreading our doubt, while strengthening our disempowering belief systems, and enrolling others in their alleged veracity, all while programming our realities accordingly.

> *We are what we pretend to be, so we must be careful about what we pretend to be.*
>
> **– Kurt Vonnegut**

People respond to the cues we give them. When we communicate with confidence and decisiveness, others are far more likely to respond in kind, and to offer their support accordingly.

Example no. 1:

We're trying to move forward with this free energy project, says the visionary entrepreneur pitching an investor his latest venture.

The proclamation is weak. Weighty with effort. Burdened by blocks, red tape, chaos and all the other logistical complications this unfortunately placed *try* implies. The declaration inspires neither confidence, nor the inclination to invest in the project. The pitch falls flat, the message doesn't land, and a giant opportunity has been bungled.

Yay, *try.*

Feel into the difference between the aforementioned sentence, and its obvious QL hack:

We are moving forward with this free energy project.

Communicated so definitively, it's easy to lend our confidence to the speaker's vision. Confidence is embedded in the transmission. This is how we build consensus for our ideas and our offerings - by languaging them in as successful and *Hell, yes!* a manner as possible, so as to magnetize aligned allies, mountain-movers and miracle-makers vibrating at a similar frequency.

This is not to deny the challenges that may very well come along with launching a new venture. Rather, it is to embrace them - the stumbles, the false starts and the frustrations - as *part of* the success process. It is to compassionately integrate this very allowing into our communication, as well as our worldview, and to claim our sometimes chaotic, meandering, non-linear processes as steps along the path to our triumphs.

Remember, our words are the fundamental building blocks that comprise this thoroughly subjective reality we are together cocreating. This means that when we decide that navigating obstacles while launching our free energy initiative is simply part of the process of launching a successful free energy initiative, and we name it as such, it is.

au · thor · i · ty, *n.*
the power or right to make decisions

Despite any and all cultural conditioning to the contrary, authority has nothing to do with hierarchy. It is not something we must earn. It is not bestowed upon us by an external source.

Authority is our natural birthright.

Quantum Languaging invites us to claim our authority with our every word; and to author our lives and our world as kindly, compassionately and anything-ly as we want to.

Example no. 2:

I'm trying to give up coffee.

We can all relate, can't we? Coffee is awesome. Coffee is also super, very habit-forming; and habits require heroic amounts of courage, strength, tenacity, patience and willpower to relinquish. Why make it harder on ourselves by tethering our efforts to words that invite half-assed results, while implying effort and challenge? Why shoot ourselves in the proverbial feet before giving ourselves the chance to soar? Why perv our quantum fields with unneccessary baggage? _Try_ sabotages our commitment to giving up coffee straight out of the gate, and allows us to entertain the possibility of failure (i.e. drinking coffee), which exponentially increases the likelihood of us chugging down a double espresso with lunch.

When I language my commitment to give up coffee in the definitive affirmative, without tossing "try" into the mix (i.e. _I am giving up coffee_), there is no room for failure to enter my consciousness. A language of definitive confidence fuels our determination, and bolsters our efforts. Words encoded with inevitable triumph do wonders to foster our resolve when we are on a deadline, and dragging ass, and jonesing for a jolt of java to perk us up, and kick us into gear.

Now, the obvious QL hack here is: *I'm giving up coffee*, which - sure, communicates the commitment without any unneccessary linguistic baggage. Sort of. Because in saying *I am giving up coffee*, the speaker is dragging out the process - clinging to the addiction she is allegedly relinquishing. It's an appropriate communication when we really, truly are struggling with caffeine withdrawal, and are choosing to be transparent, and possibly inviting support; and yet, it's still not our best choice.

I gave up coffee is stronger, in that it proclaims the habit's completion, thus languaging any lingering cravings or withdrawal symptoms out of the conversation, as well as our present moment reality. Remember, our physiology *responds* to our thoughts and our words, which means we are infinitely more likely to be affected by the physical symptoms of caffeine withdrawal when we speak them into our present moment experience. *I gave up coffee* is still steeped in the past, and tethered to the addiction from which we claim to be free. If this is where we are in our process, this is a perfectly appropriate way to language it, while *I don't drink coffee* is really, truly our strongest Quantum Languaging hack, in its temporal sovereignty, as well as its simple, honest precision.

All this is to say: *Do not try; do.*

can't

Can't. Ugh.

I mean, sure; there are a handful of situations and circumstances where *can't* is entirely appropriate; but - trust me - they are infinitely fewer and farther between than its ubiquitous usage suggests. Now, I don't want to go mucking with my quantum field by drumming up a litany of examples that would otherwise limit my expansion/evolution/awesomeness, but think of physically/logistically prohibitive situations, as in: *I can't grow a beard; I can't lift this twelve-ton Jeep; I can't meet you in Sri Lanka for dinner because I'm in Ojai;* or - quite simply - *I can't hear you; it's really loud in this zero gravity chamber.*

Alas, it's not the exceptions that disempower us; it's the unconscious overuse of this wee little contraction that steals our sovereignty and our power, thus allowing us to languish in victimhood, and all the life-squelching stagnation its energetic frequency engenders.

When we say that we *can't,* we give our power away - to a system, a human, a distorted relationship to time; to any number of energies, entities or misconceptions that don't actually have any power over us, in and of themselves, unless we choose to give it to them.

Example:

I can't hike today; I have to work.

The proclamation implies a state of powerlessness that has us enslaved to our job, and our circumstances, while claiming we have no choice in the matter. Except, we do. As sovereign beings, we can absolutely choose to play hooky, and the hit the trails with our friend. Sure, our actions will likely inspire consequences that might lose us wages, pro-motions or job security, to say nothing of the potential damages to our reputations, relationships and checking accounts; but, to claim we *can't* is to thoroughly deny our sovereign power to make these choices for ourselves. *Can't*, in this context, is wholly inaccurate, as well as extremely damaging to the speaker's authority, and personal empowerment.

In opting for the Quantum Languaging hack: *I'm working today; let's hike on Thursday,* we get to honor our free will, while owning our responsibil-ity for our choices. It is a helpful and empowering reframe that allows us to see the benefits of choosing to work (i.e. having shelter, running water and plenty of raw chocolate in the cupboard) over taking the day off, which allows us to show up in good spirits, and gratitude.

When we say we *can't*, we deny the responsibility inextricably bound to incarnation, adulthood and planetary citizenry, instead giving our power away to any number of unspecified, imaginary others. Except these imaginary others don't exist. I mean, sure; TSA agents exist, as do the rules they are employed to enforce - the ones about traveling with sharp, stabby things and however-many ounces of liquid-like substances, which means that to say: *I can't bring that fig jam you love with me on this trip, Grandma* is both accurate and appropriate. Except, now that I think about it, it isn't really; because I can choose to check my bag, and thus pack the five ounces of jam in a big ol' suitcase I pay them to put under the plane. Except I'm only staying the weekend, while also saving for a Tesla, which makes checking a bag seem rather impractical; which is all to say: *I'm not going to bring the jam this time, Grandma.*

Codependent No More

It can be a little jarring at first - claiming responsibility for rejecting someone else's request, while not blaming external circumstances by couching our Nos in the word can't. Still, to deny our authority to protect another's feelings is a codependent cop-out. Who am I to assume that Grandma can't handle my choice to not bring her jam? And if my no ruffles Grandma's feathers, good; because that's just the sort of trigger that - when held loosely, and mined for treasure - allows us to grow our emotional intelligence, while taking responsibility for our feelings and our experiences without needing others to protect them on our behalf. This is how we cultivate wholeness, independence, autonomy and healthy boundaries. How's that for high-vibe multitasking?

Quantum Languaging hacks for *can't:*

am not available for

not going to

choosing to/not to

> **Quantum Languaging Hacking Tip**
>
> *Get creative with the QL hacks. Play. Find the just-right words and phrases that feel resonant for you. The shifts might feel awkward at first, given that we are breaking patterns while carving out previously uncharted neural pathways and forging new communication strategies. Let's let it be awkward, and let it be weird, while honoring ourselves for being brave enough to ditch our disempowering languaging patterns, and hacking our communication strategies in service to our most expanded, empowered selves, as well as the (infinitely upleveled) world at large.*

have to

Did you really think I was going to let that slide – the whole *I can't hike today; I have to work* example I put forth in the previous section? *As if.*

Have to vibrates at a similar frequency as *can't,* in that it mistakenly denies our sovereignty and our free will. There is nothing we *have to* do. Everything is a choice. Some choices inspire consequences that don't necessarily serve our highest good, which means we are wise to make different choices. I don't *have to* go to work, I **choose** to go to work because I choose to have a steady income, and the structure that a job provides, because it allows me to be more effective in my creative life, and to take care of myself in the ways that I value. I don't *have to* wake up early to meditate; it is a choice that serves me by allowing me to ground, and center, and quiet my mind before I tackle the day. I don't *have to* call my mother, I choose to because it fosters our connection, and gives her a chance to tell me about all the terrible things she watched on the news last night, as well as how much ass she's kicking in Pilates. In owning our decisions, instead of feigning obligation, we empower ourselves as con-scious creators by claiming our every choice as a coherent and aligned step that – together with all the others – supports us in manifesting our dreams, achieving our destinies and living joyful, connected, abundant lives while changing our world for the way, way better.

Quantum Languaging hacks for *have to*:

am going to

choosing to

am committed to

get to

Next-Level Contemplation Fodder:

Victim-Schmictim

Habitually employed words and phrases like *can't, have to* and other responsibility-shirkers point to an underlying victim consciousness informing our languaging patterns. This bizarre cultural diversion has reached epidemic proportions, baiting us to fight over whose subgroup is more marginalized than the others', and to cordon ourselves off into separate categories based on race, religion, gender, skin color, ability, disability, ideology, sexual preference, political affiliation, and any and all associated combinations thereof. So divided, we train ourselves to look for subgroup affronts, thus focusing our attention on affront collection, which ultimately increases the likelihood of manifesting affrontal[5] experiences, because that's how reality creation works: attention determines experience; we attract what we focus on.

> *What you think about, you bring about.*
>
> — Napolean Hill

And so it is that we arm ourselves with affront tales, and affront statistics, all so we can prove that our subgroup is the most marginalized subgroup of them all, and deserves the most sympathy, because we - as a

---

5   **affrontal**; *adj.* having or marked by the quality of affront

collective - are under the very misguided impression that there is value in pity, and that the biggest victim wins.

Our lexicon is lousy with disempowering languaging patterns that stem from this unexamined belief - that there is value in victimhood, and in the sympathy this orientation supposedly merits. Except, there isn't. Like, not even a drop. New paradigm mojo lies in empowerment – in sovereignty, and free will, and in the truth of our omniscopic awesomeness, which gives not one single shit about meaningless statistics that profess that we are less than, or that we are owed a big, walloping batch of worthless pity for the marginalized status that we, as new p. badasses, and planetary superheroes, don't buy into for a single, solitary second.

Quantum Languaging Somatics

From a safe, settled place of grounded stillness[6], say both of these sentences out loud, pausing to feel into the visceral associations that come along with each:

I have to go to work.

I get to go to work.

I don't know about you, but for me, *have to* inspires feelings of constriction, restriction, contraction and resentment. Rebel consciousness runs deep in my DNA, and as soon as I *have to* do anything, my entire being seizes up, my free will digs in its heels, and my preferences freak way out – a process which has historically proven really energetically inefficient when getting my *have tos* done.

Conversely, *get to* inspires feelings of joy and excitement, regardless of what activity the words are modifying. Sure, it's a bit of a Jedi mind-trick

---

6   Three deep belly breaths are fabulous to this end.

to language certain commitments with a sunshine-y "get to;" and that's the point! We are, all of us, making this life thing up as we go along – including culture and language and attitude – and, we get to make the whole ride as fun and easy and joyful as we choose. Reframing our choices in ways that empower and uplift lightens the collective load while modeling empowered wonderfulness for our fellow humans.

can

Let's go back to *can't* for a moment. Deductive reasoning would have us believe that *can* is a perfectly adequate upgrade for *can't*. The thing is, deductive reasoning is a narrow pathway of perception that very often neglects subtler and more nuanced energetic factors, and that – in this case, at least – isn't serving us.

Can is a conceptual abstraction that speaks to what might be possible in the future. *Can* is evasive. *Can* is an effective way to avoid responsibility, and to dodge commitment. *Can* stands still, marveling at its potential while the world whizzes by.

Example:

"Together," declares Imaginary US President X, "we can make America a great, thriving bastion of peace, unity and prosperity for all."

It's a lovely assertion. Bold. Bright. High-vibing and inclusive. Except it's also weak and wishy-washy and evasive, because it is steeped in the future-projected potential that POTUS doesn't have the balls to claim – for himself, or the nation he's supposed to be leading. It's true, sure. Together, we *can* do this. But, *will* we? There's not a lot of action in this sentence. It's conjecture. It's conversation. It's masturbation. What it's not, is a commitment. And this is not to criticize conversation ripe with potential and promise and visions of a rad future, rather it is to say that to move ourselves forward, and to show up for this peaceful (r)evolution we are together leading, we are well-served by decisive languaging that gets us off our asses, out of the cozy realms of future-predicated possibility, and into the realized frequency and *is*-ness of the new, **now**.

> *The secret of change is to focus all of your energy, not on fighting the old, but on building the new.*
>
> **- Socrates**

The game plan will follow the claim. It's okay if we don't (yet) know the *how*. The *hows* trail the commitment. Our job is to be brave enough to declare the intention, and trust that we will attract the *hows* by staying steadfastly committed to the aim.

Quantum Languaging hacks for *can*:

will

am going to

am committed to

am

Next-Level Contemplation Fodder:

Commitment

What is your relationship to commitment? Pay attention to your languaging choices around scheduling, and making plans. What do they reflect as far as your willingness to commit, and your tendency to keep your commitments?

Track your communication patterns to get a clearer picture of your relationship to commitment. Observe without judgment. There is no right. There is no wrong. You are simply collecting data from the standpoint of a neutral observer. With this in mind, feel into whether your relationship to commitment is serving your highest potential, and your dharmic path. If it isn't, what steps are you willing to take to shift it?

will

But Dani, you protest, *you just said* will *is the wiser choice for* can!

It's true. I did. And, it is. Sort of. On one level, *will* vibrates with the conviction that *can* lacks. Still, it remains a dilly-dally word that speaks to the promise of future action, rather than present moment embodiment. *Will* puts off for tomorrow what we are fully capable of doing today. Sure, there are circumstances in which *will* is appropriate, and on point, as in: *Next month, I will be giving a TED Talk in Barcelona.* At the same time, there are lots of circumstances wherein *will* allows us to procrastinate, and drag our feet, while shying away from our greatness.

Example:

We will put an end to institutionalized racism in this country, the leader of the free world promises during her State of the Union address.

It sounds like a solid commitment, right? Er...not really, because in languaging this timely, idealistic and *no-duh* pledge this way, our free world leader, as well as those of us who comprise the "we" she references, get to sidestep any and all present moment execution of said pledge, and to put it off, indefinitely. Employing *will* in this way weakens the commitment, verily draining it of any and all mojo. *Will* doesn't galvanize action. It inspires thumb-twiddling, rug-shoving and status quo. Sure, it *sounds* committed, while allowing us to silently surrender our sovereign authority to embody and institute equality *now*, and to sell-out our vision to a faraway, someday future that may or may not ever actually come.

Feel the strength and conviction of the QL hacked version of our original pledge:

We are putting an end to institutionalized racism in this country.

Powerful, right? In languaging this statement in the present, we move from *aiming* to take action, to *taking* action. **Now.**

> **Quantum Reality-Shaping Reminder:**
> *Let us remember that every moment carries with it the opportunity for change – for a different choice, an alternative perspective, a single step forged upon a previously uncharted path. Change is not something that happens tomorrow. Change happens because we make different choices today.*

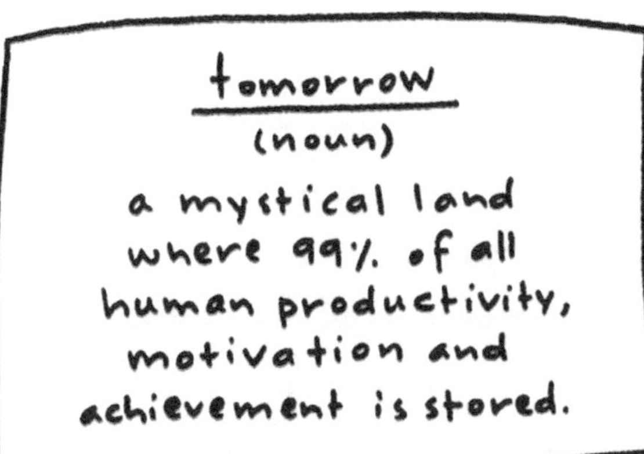

but

But is a brick wall, a scowling hand in a smiling face and a whopping energetic *No. But* brings the momentum of collaboration to a screeching halt by denying that which inspired it. *But* is a combative little conjunction with a Napoleonic complex, tethered to an unconscious need to be right.

Whether we are brainstorming nuclear disarmament inside a twelve-person think tank, or figuring out which appetizer to split with our besties, we are all wise to master the art of collaboration, not (just) because we are an interdependent species necessarily reliant upon each other to sustain a vibrant and harmonious planet, but because it's way more fun to work together. Did you catch that? Did you see what that *but* just did? How, so-placed, it elevates the veracity of *fun* over that now, seemingly secondary, if not entirely irrelevant *vibrant and harmonious Earth game sustaining piece?*

But suggests that the idea that follows is somehow more relevant, more accurate and more wonderful than the idea that precedes it. These illusions of hierarchy and separation are old p. distortions that take a notable toll on the collaborative process, when the truth is: all perspectives are valuable, if only for the energies they trigger and the reflections they inspire. To this end, we are served by languaging that acknowledges the value of the ideas preceding it, while augmenting the possibilities with the ones that follow.

Quantum Languaging hacks for *but*:

and

still

yet

also

plus

while

as well

Next-Level Contemplation Fodder:

Acknowledgment

Acknowledgment vibrates at a most magical frequency in that it soothes oopsies and ouchies, opens both hearts and doors, and deepens intimacy while cultivating trust, respect and warm fuzzies for all involved.

All suffering wants is to be felt. Acknowledgment soothes our suffering in saying:

Yes, pain; I see you.

Yes, humiliation/hurt feelings/abandonment issues, I recognize you.

That very recognition is our succor, and – ultimately - our redemption.

May we be brave enough to acknowledge the suffering we see, and the pain we inflict – upon others, as well as ourselves.

need

Need implies lack. In fact, it screams lack at the top of its invisible little lungs – shrieking in desperation, while off-gassing scarcity, instability and wide-eyed grasping for infinite life rafts with day-old mascara running down her cheeks. *Need's* dramatic (if invisible) histrionics repel precisely that which it craves in affirming what *isn't,* and – as we've already established - vibrating at the frequency of lack.

Scarcity-speak (i.e. languaging that affirms *not-havingness*) is a tricky, sticky communication pattern that only works against us when it comes to manifesting our dreams and wantings. Remember, the subconscious mind doesn't grok nuance, and is super, very literal when it comes to interpreting words as reality-creation commands that it then – in concert with natural law and cosmic forces - translates into reality/experience. So, when we allege to *need* something, we are not just declaring lack, we are asking for more of it, while inadvertently pushing away whatever it is we claim to *need.*

When I *say: I need a new couch,* I am not only confirming the existential distance between myself and the turquoise velvet chaise I'd really like to have, I am engulfed in the vibrational frequency of lack. So immersed, this frequency instructs the universe to keep any and all cozy, scrumptious blue-green sofas out of reach, devoted as said infinite intelligence is to meeting my vibration.

I am so excited to take a nap on my new couch.

It is wiser, and way more effective to language our so-called "needs" in the declarative/affirmative, because when embedded in the frequency of *already-having,* they have a tendency to manifest all the more quickly, and easily.

Quantum Languaging Hacks for *need*:

am blessed to have/use/meet/et al

choose/am choosing

invite/am inviting

am so excited to have/use/meet/et al

Next-Level Contemplation Fodder:

The Art of Manifestation + the Illusion of Linear Time

For a lot of us, it feels really weird to speak about *having* and *enjoying* and *being super, very excited about* the things we are still in the process of manifesting.

Are we lying? Faking it? Fooling ourselves into some sort of woo-woo magical thinking?

Not. At. All.

> *We are living in a culture entirely hypnotized by the illusion of time.*
>
> — Alan Watts

The real-deal truth of the matter is that we live in a reality comprised of infinite possibility. There is a boundless array of experiences we can choose to experience in our lifetime. To hone in on any one of these wantings in the otherwise dizzying sea of infinite available options means that, on some level, this reality **already exists**. Remember that time is omnidirectional and simultaneous. This means that – outside of the third dimension, where time appears to be linear – there is no past, and there is no future. Rather, all possibilities and experiences are happening at the same "time," on multiple dimensions at once. So, for us to tap into a desire, or a consistent longing in *this* dimension, means that – on some level – it is already happening.

Quantum Languaging teaches us to collapse the dimensional distance between our wants and our now by using words encoded with the frequencies of *havingness*, because Quantum Langauging is awesome.

want

And so we move from *need* to *want*, cleverly deducing that *want* makes for a fine Quantum Languaging hack when referencing that which we are inviting into our experience. Except, it doesn't.

Want, while stronger in that it tones down *need's* victimy vibes, summoning the will and the courage to lay claim to its desires, still separates us from that which we are calling in. When we *want* something, we are (still) reinforcing the fact that we don't have it; and thus, pushing it farther away.

More effective is a languaging hack that allows us to name that which we are calling in, and to lay claim to its materialization without affirming lack, or confusing whomever we're speaking to about our actual havingness in the process.

And so, instead of *wanting* a new car, I *choose* a new car. I *am excited* to drive my comfortable new car. I *am ready for* a safe, new, fuel-efficient, fun-to-drive car. I am *inviting* the arrival of my indigo blue Tesla station wagon, with the sunroof, the tan interior, and the surround sound speakers.

Quantum Languaging hacks for *want*:

choose
invite
love
welcome
am calling in
am grateful for
am excited about/to receive
am

Next-Level Contemplation Fodder:

The Extraordinary Power of I Am:
I am are the most powerful words in all the mystical traditions.
Encoded in these words is the transformative power of the
~~universe~~ multiverse.

Yes, really.

When it comes to stating our intentions, and aligning ourselves
with what we want to give, receive, achieve, emanate, resonate,
experience and share, these little words - I am - are our quickest,
and most effective manifestation shortcut.

On Claiming Our Desires, and Being Very, Super Specific

Desire gets a bad rap in our culture. Good, spiritual people are supposed to have transcended the stuff. *Wanting* gets confused with greed, which gets ascribed to assholes[7], and corporate overlords with vested interests in any number of nefarious/earth rapey industries. Plus, it's way cooler to feign asceticism, or indifference.

I dunno, shrugs Allegedly Enlightened Dude X when presented with a choice between Yerba Maté or Oolong tea. *It doesn't matter. Whatever.*

---

7   The truth is we're all assholes; and, we're all saints - the whole messy, wonderful lot of us.

On the one hand, he's right – nothing matters. On the other hand, this moment is, in fact, the ONLY thing that could possibly matter; so, why not claim it, and all the meaning and visceral mojo it portends, by creating it for maximum enjoyability? Why not get present, and decide to give a shit about whether we want an antioxidant-rich brain high, or the earthy energetic buzz that comes along with black tea? Why not take responsibility for our experience by choosing for ourselves how we want it to feel, and what we want it to taste like?

The starting point of all achievement is desire.

— **Napolean Hill**

There is nothing, nothing wrong with allowing ourselves the luxury of experience, and cultivating a healthy desire for said experience. In fact, honing in on our genuine desires is a pretty gosh-darned crucial step on the path to achieving our destiny, and realizing our full potential. And, it's especially necessary now, when so many of us are unhappy with the direction the world seems to be going, and have yet to put forth an alternate vision that will more effectively serve the greatest good for our planet, and all the beings inhabiting it. How are we going to figure this stuff out if we don't tap into how we **want** it to look, feel and function?

To this end, putting time and effort into pinpointing our greatest desires is an essential exercise for anyone wanting to live an authentic, realized life. For some, that might mean living off the land, fermenting biodynamic vegetables, and whittling; for others, it will mean crunching numbers, overhauling the jury selection process, and practicing Krav Maga on the weekends. It is not an abuse of privilege to dream biggest. It is, however, an affront to the universe, and to our privilege and our blessings not to. The Earth game is an abundant playground of infinite possibility. How do **you** want to play your version?

Quantum Languaging/Living Practice:

You are hereby invited to take yourself on a daydream date. Carve out some time that allows for spaciousness, expansion and some languid lollygagging, and let your mind wander. What does your dream life look like? Where do you live? What sort of structure do you call home? What color are the walls? What sort of people do you spend your time with? What do you do for work? For fun? For self-care? What are your hobbies? How do you feel when you climb into bed at night? What kind of sheets are you wrapped in, and what sorts of sounds lull you to sleep?

Get specific. The more specific you get, the easier it is for the universe to deliver, and the less room there is for it to fill in your blanks for you with stuff you might not really, truly want. Like that time I manifested a Hollywood Hills guest house, but forgot to mention that said dream digs were clean and safe and quiet, and ended up with raucous neighbors, a peeping Tom and a cockroach infestation. Lesson learned. Details rock.

should

Should is a bossy little word that vibrates at a despotic, tyrannical frequency, declaring that it knows best, while instantly shutting down the receiver, and rendering whatever messages that follow it mute. Way to go, *should*.

You should apply for a Rhoades Scholarship, says someone who cares about us, and thinks we're smart.

It's wise advice, and a great idea, except the problem is, we didn't actually hear it, because the meat of the matter was muffled in the wake of the preceding *should.* In fact, the instant *should* was aspirated through the speaker's lips, our every fractal cell contracted, while an invisible pair of hands clamped down around our throats, and the words that trailed its well-intended heels sounded like the unintelligible blathering of every adult in every Peanuts holiday cartoon.

Call it ego, rebel consciousness or Uranus' presence in our solar system, but humans have a tendency to shut down when being told what to do. This means we aren't actually available to hear what very well may be great advice hidden inside the frequency of an unconsciously dropped *should*. It's unfortunate given how ubiquitous the word is, and how much good, great, brilliant advice may very well follow it. As long as we are expending the energy to communicate our ideas, doesn't it make sense to language them in such a way that we're actually heard?

Quantum Languaging hacks for *should*:

Are you open to considering

Another option to consider is

might want to consider

would be wise to consider

a wiser choice might be

can

(absolutely no) absolutes

Ye Ol' Ego

Before we dig into the deleterious downsides of absolutes, let us take a moment to talk about our friend, the ego.

Everyone's got one – a (supposedly) separate self comprised of wounds, traumas, shadows, limiting beliefs and lies. This false personality construct yammering in our heads all day, every day is utterly devoted to being right, and to convincing us that we are separate from our fellow humans, which – as we already know – is bullshit.

To this end, when the ego hears an absolute, it immediately busies itself with the task of proving said absolute (as well as the speaker) wrong, which means that while we are ever so eloquently delivering any number of poignant, visionary insights into genetic coding, or consciousness hacking, or Kim-chi for breakfast, we have already lost the attention, and thus the ear, of he who is now straining his brain to find the exception to the implied rule that is the *never* we carelessly dropped a couple sentences back.

Oy vey, the ego.

About Those Absolutes...

Never and *always* are temporal cages, impossible promises, dramatic bursts of hyperbole that chip away at the authenticity of the experiences we are communicating. Let us remember that we are all-powerful creators, working in constant concert with the universe to design our every moment, as well as the world as we know it. As such, *never* and *always* are imaginary limitations we place upon ourselves that carry on for inadvertent eternities.

"I never win," Molly whines after losing yet another racquetball game.

The thing is, *never* is a really long time. And while Molly may not have won yet, in opting for a dramatic and exaggerated assessment of her ~~losing streak~~ *learning curve*, she is anchoring the perceived failure ever deeper into her psyche, as well as into the morphogenetic field[8] at large. In saying she "never" wins, Molly is choosing to set her personal vibration to the frequency of *loser*, while instructing the Universe to sustain this supposed losing streak with which she is identifying into infinity and beyond. Duly charged, the universe will inevitably respond by directing space, time and material reality to configure to support Molly's statement.

---

8   the invisible web of consciousness/field of habit, behavior and experience that links the entire human race, as well as every being on the planet.

Never and *always* create massive blocks, verily negating the possibility of change or growth with their (very) lengthy temporal implications. These absolutes dig in their heels, while stubbornly claiming permanence, which is sort of super ridiculous, given that one of the hallmarks of this whole Earth game is that everything - even the sun, the moon and the sea - will, eventually, die. Everything changes, even Molly's (alleged) losing streak.

I always get lost in this neighborhood.

What a great way to continue the pattern, and to avoid actually learning to master navigating the area in question. When we employ *always* (as well as *never*), we project our past onto our future, inadvertently crafting our very own perpetual status quo, an everlasting sameness that bolsters our egos in proving us right, and keeping us stagnant.

It is infinitely more empowering to language our patterns in such a way that we stay open to the growth, change and miracles we are calling in by choosing words that acknowledge the perceived consistency of the behavior while availing ourselves to a different experience.

Quantum Languaging hacks for *never*:

haven't yet

haven't historically

am looking forward to

am excited to

Quantum Languaging hacks for *always*:

often

sometimes

am prone to

have (had) a tendency to

have, historically

have, in the past

maybe, might, possibly, perhaps
(and other instances of *non-committal nothing speak*)

Maybe is limbo. *Possibly* is purgatory. *Perhaps* is a wishy-washy hook forged of indefinite indecisiveness, and dandelion fluff.

The sabotage is two-fold. When we are asked a question, be it: *Do you want to go to dinner tonight?*, *Would you write me a book blurb?*, or *Will the blueprints be finished by Monday?*, and we answer with the colossally non-committal *Maybe*, we are not only unconsciously preventing those to whom we are speaking from moving forward[9], we are choosing stagnation for ourselves.

As relates to she who is on the receiving end of any one of these fence-riding replies, it's just plain rude, as this kind of languaging functions to keep others open and available for our potential *Yeses*, while still holding onto *No* as a distinct possibility. And sure, there are plenty of situations wherein non-committal languaging points to an authentic juncture in our process, and isn't all that inconveniencing; and yet, at their vibrational core, these fence-riders are subtle, manipulative power plays that keep our questioners in the dark as to the authentic status of our Venn diagram of engaging.

---

9   or, at the very least, attempting to

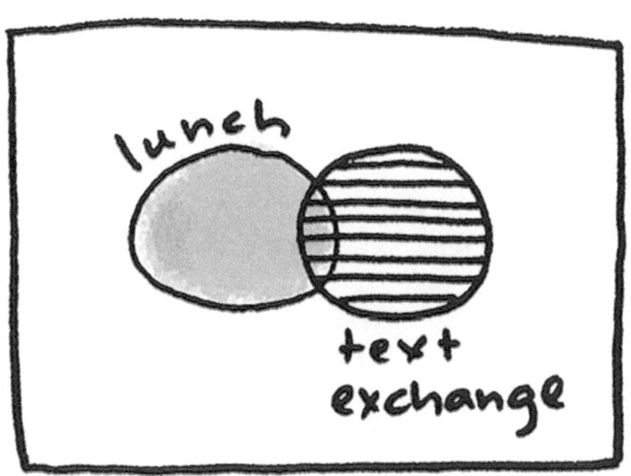

For the speaker herself, it's flat-out self-sabotage. Our casually dropped *maybes* keep us bound to any number of dangling possibilities, to potential pathways that nibble our energy, while sapping our focus, our attention and our power.

Open Loops

An open loop is a type of energy leak that – without hard deadlines, or finite boundaries to define it – depletes us. Non-committal languaging endeavors to keep our energy kind of, sort of available to any number of potentials, which drain our psychic space on multiple levels. It's hardly an efficient means of engaging the world, to say nothing of the fun and exciting mission of steering our planet onto an infinitely more harmonious and sustainable trajectory – a rather pressing task that is inviting our undivided attention, as well as the full scope of our mental faculties.

All this is to say: Close them loops, yo. Decisiveness rocks.

Quantum Languaging hacks for *non-committal nothing speak:*

Yes
No
I'll get back to you on that by ____________ (insert day and time-range here)

if

Oh, *if*...wherever shall we begin?

For starters, it's a lolly-gagger. *If* is yet another non-committal fence-riding word. Except, *if* doesn't stop with the dilly-dallying, decision-procrastinating thing. No, *if* likes to multi-task, introducing a whole host of distractions, interruptions and potential apocalyptic *anythings* into our collective fields of possibility, only to inadvertently deter our stated aims. *If* entertains notions of failure, flakiness and worst case scenarios, attempting to play it safe in the cozy comfort zone of future-projected possibility, wondering *if* something outside itself is going to nudge said possibility into existence. *If* is passive and weak, readily relinquishing the speaker's power to an imaginary authority, or a string of theoretical circumstances that may arbitrarily allow it permission to be. Or not. *Whatevs.*

Example no. 1:

I'll be really happy if my book gets published, says Not Super Committed Writer X.

Do you feel how disempowering the statement is? Aside from the glaring issue that is the condition the speaker is choosing to place on his very own happiness (*Uh...hello, limiting belief!*), there is this nebulous question mark that he himself is attaching to the final outcome of his passion project. If the author isn't certain of his book's destiny, how can we reasonably expect anyone else to put their faith into it?[10]

Remember, time is multi-dimensional, and what *can be* **already is** on some layer of existence. Instead of waiting for something to manifest to feel worthy of naming it, Quantum Languaging invites us to be bold enough to claim the *is*-ness of our visions *first*, and *then* follow the breadcrumbs of signs, synchronicities and intuition to materialize them. And so it is that we grab hold of our dreams and our visions with *when*, acknowledging that they already **are**, while inviting the Universe to show us the way.

I'll be really happy when my book gets published, says Quantum Languaging Student/Emerging Author Q.

Oh, really? we poke, because every word matters, and it's super helpful to have a tribe of Quantum Languaging savvy peaceful (r)evolutionaries at the ready to point our attention toward our blind spots.

Clear, Cancel, Delete, Emerging Author says, catching the conditional, future-projected emotion as it leaves his lips. *I am absolutely happy and*

---

10   This is an instance where *if* is serving a valuable, exemplary and neutrally-vibrating function. Do you feel the difference between this use of *if*, and the one in the example we are considering?

whole, now; and, I am also going to be really super excited when my book gets published.

Well done, Grasshopper.

Obviously, there are lots of instances where *if* is thoroughly appropriate – like when it comes to logistics, or those very real instances when we don't have enough information to commit to a definitive outcome. Exceptions abound. Still, what we are referring to here are those timid, doubting *ifs* that chip away at our power, our confidence and our devotion to the highest possible outcomes, regardless of the challenges that may or may not present themselves along the way.

Example no. 2:

Give me a call if you're inspired, Jake says to Emma, who might very well be the mother of his unborn children.

If, in this instance, puts forth the possibility that Emma won't be inspired to reach out. It seeds the lack of inspiration that may or may not be authentic to Emma's experience. Connecting with folks is challenging enough in the digital age. Why exacerbate any potential roadblocks to intimacy by willingly dropping doubt into the mix? Why not assume the best, and speak to and from that reality – an action that happens to be contagious, and will likely inspire Emma to assume the best herself, and – with any luck – get these two potential lovebirds on the phone.

Give me a call when you're inspired, Jake says to Emma, who is suddenly warm, and tingly, and a little bit flustered – attracted as she is to confident, self-assured men named Jake.

Quantum Languaging hack for *if*:

when

just

Our deepest fear is not that we are inadequate. Our deepest fear is that we are powerful beyond measure. It is our light, not our darkness, that most frightens us.

– Marianne Williamson

An offshoot of the verb *justify*, *just* is a useless modifier employed to downplay the wonderfulness it would otherwise be referencing, rationalizing its shrunken stature with down-turned eyes and inward pointing feet, hoping you won't judge the ideas that follow it.

I love this drawing! Art Lover Q enthuses.

It's just a study, explains Insecure Artist X, simultaneously shrugging off the compliment, while explaining why any and all negative judgments you are(n't even) harboring are totally unwarranted.

In this instance, *just* clearly points to an inability to receive. The shadow affects Insecure Artist X in all the obvious ways, while fueling the self-esteem issues informing it. The issue also impacts Art Lover Q, as *just*, employed in this manner, is a way of explaining that she is wrong, and that she has shitty taste in art, and that she should shut her dumb cake hole, *hasta pronto*-like.

Just weakens the nouns and verbs it modifies – taking the whole lot of descriptives that trail it down a few notches, lest they get too full of themselves. The problem is that playing small is an old p. survival strategy that isn't doing us any favors. Dimming our light to make ourselves more likeable is an affront to our talent, our blessings and our unique genius. Let us instead shine big and bright, emboldened by the knowledge that our sparkle ignites magic in others; and that when we are - all of us - vibing high and humble, and real and confident on our and each other's wonderfulness, we really, truly are invincible.

Quantum Languaging hack for *just*:

Uh...just don't use it.

sorry

They're ubiquitous, these thoughtless *sorries* needlessly insinuating themselves into our daily doings, inadvertently sprinkling soggy bits of sorrow all over our sneakers, and our world. The word is incessantly misused - offered as a question when we're not sure we heard someone correctly, and sputtered in countless awkward moments during which we have no idea what else to say. *Sorry* is, in fact, so overused, that when offered as an actual apology, it's pretty much meaningless.

"*Sorry,*" blurts the woman exiting the public restroom, seemingly startled to see me waiting on the other side of it.

For what, exactly, are you apologizing? I want to ask. For peeing? For getting to the toilet before I did? For washing your hands, and re-applying your lip-gloss? And, if you're apologizing for something as benign as emerging from a public washroom, then how am I to trust the 'Sorry' you utter when you apologize for canceling lunch plans, or spilling cranberry juice on my blouse? How will I know you're truly sorry when it's clear you don't know what the word means, or when it's appropriate to use it?

In addition to the grossly misused exclamatory model, there are the *sorries* we offer in response to someone else's loss or challenge. *Sorry* employed in this capacity enables us in taking co-dependent responsibility for other people's feeling states, as though we are somehow to blame for their torn meniscus, or their mother's dementia, or that speeding ticket they got en route to Big Sur. These reckless, ill-fitting *sorries* speak to our collective discomfort in the space of shared shadows – a culturally-rampant experience we are wise to sift out from under our proverbial rug, and look at, and shift, if for no other reason than how else are we going to grow our emotional intelligence, and learn to get along as a single, unified species?

Quantum Languaging hacks for *Sorry*:

Surprise!

This Quantum Languaging hack is inspired by my friend, and self-proclaimed *Yesologist*, Justin. Instead of *Sorry*, he says (okay, hollers) *Surprise!* The theory is that *Surprise* acknowledges the oopsie, while shifting the energetic inclination from shame, embarrassment or disappointment to levity, laughter and celebration. As we mentioned earlier, it is the magical healing frequency of acknowledgment that truly dissipates the ouch of human interaction gone awry. *Surprise* allows us to acknowledge any such missteps with lightness and joy, thus vibrating these frequencies far and wide.

Thank you

When I observe the urge to apologize (which is so often a cleverly disguised excuse to self-flagellate), I will instead offer a simple *Thank you,* which serves to acknowledge the person for showing up as a valuable reflection in service to my/our growth.

Congratulations

When someone loses something - a job, a house, a boyfriend, a testicle - I tend to go with: *Congratulations!* followed by an enthusiastic: *Way to shake up your life!*

I'm not trying to barrel over their pain or their process; rather, I am offering a different perspective. Life is change. Endings herald new beginnings. It is, of course, crucial to grieve the losses as they come, while it is just as important to acknowledge the space that opens up in the process, as well as all the possibilities said space portends.

Part 3

Idioms, Expressions, Check-Outs
+ Other Communication Habits To Avoid

Negative Space Speak

In order to change an existing paradigm, you do not struggle to try and change the problematic model. You create a new model, and make the old one obsolete.

— Buckminster Fuller

Have you noticed how much time we spend talking about what *isn't* happening, and what we *don't* want? Ask a guy to describe his dream girl, and he will likely tell you what turns him off. Or, if you're me, ask your mom where she wants to go for lunch, and you'll get an earful about how much she hated that raw, vegan place you roped her into going to for your birthday. We Westerners have this silly habit of rambling on (and on) about what isn't working in the world – the jobs we can't get, the sex no one's having, the art we're not making and the politicians we didn't elect. It's a great way to keep ourselves stuck in countless distorted and dysfunctional old p. energies, as the very act of speaking about the things that aren't working sustains the vibration of all those things that aren't working, thus strengthening their *is*-ness, as well as their hold on us.

Remember, everything is energy. Whether we praise or vilify something, we feed it with our attention, and whatever charge we place upon it. And so, regardless of our righteous intentions, when we rail against fracking, big pharma or factory farming, all we're really doing is empowering a broken paradigm forged of fear, greed and separation, while strengthening the very corruption we're referencing.

This isn't to encourage rug-shoving, face-burying or half-lidded, *S'all good* sort of spiritual bypassing. On the contrary, we must look our challenges directly in the eyes to get a clear picture of the wounds, stories and shadows at play, so that we can transmute them into gifts that make our lives, and the world at large, infinitely more wonderful. Still, we are unwise to indulge in the sport of offering endless snarky commentary about how messed up our world is(n't), because these acts only empower the entities, circumstances and situations we claim to oppose.

Plus, it's a terrific waste of time.

We transform our lives and our world by speaking better versions into existence. Let us shift our focus from what *isn't* working to what *is* working, and what *will* work even better, and to how good and great and wonderful we are making it.

Ditch the *anti*.

If you hold an anti-war rally, I shall not attend. But if you hold a pro-peace rally, invite me.

— Mother Teresa

As inspired as I am to claim that I'm anti-*anti*, it would be metahypocritical, and likely confusing, because the truth is, I don't ascribe to anti-*anything*.

This seemingly innocuous little prefix is a bastion of polarization, pitting us against whatever it modifies; creating enemies, adversaries and divisiveness whilst employing brute force in its weasly, ineffective efforts to barrel over all that it purports to rail against, which – as we've already established – only fuels the energies said prefix alleges to oppose.

Force always creates counterforce; its effect is to polarize rather than unify.

— Dr. David R. Hawkins

Take, for example, the marketing ploy that is the "anti-aging" movement, which seeks to pit our populace against time's onward ticking, and the impermanent nature of these meat suits we're all borrowing, attempting to convince countless generations of humans (read: consumers) that time is an enemy, despite the fact that a) it is a conceptual abstraction that shapes this dimensional reality; b) isn't gonna slow its roll any time soon, or ever; and c) isn't even fundamentally terrible. Aside from being a ridiculous proposition and a losing battle, this framing has us trapped in the vibrational frequency of *aging*, and all the loaded stigmas the word implies. And so we find ourselves preoccupied with our aging process, focusing our precious energy and attention on the futile task of beating it, instead of surrendering to what is, and choosing to align our frequencies with our optimized selves, and the experience of feeling amazing in our own skin.

We don't revolutionize our economy by declaring ourselves "anti-capitalist", nor do we heal our dysfunctional relationship to impermanence by declaring war on time, and then branding a zillion-and-one "anti-aging" creams, serums and treatments that demonize our sun spots and our laugh lines. We don't evolve by reacting *against* the old, rather by moving *towards* the new. We change our world by deciding how a better version looks, feels and functions, and then orienting ourselves toward nurturing the new and improved version. Tenaciously. Single-pointedly. With confidence and compassion, and a twinkle in our collective eye.

Thou Shall Not Disasterbate.

And then there's the disasterbating, wherein we give voice to our worst fears, and to the most terrible, awful possibilities imaginable, wasting our exquisite life force languishing in low-vibe bummer frequencies. It would be one thing if we were quietly running these catastrophic visions in the private confines of our own minds, wherein our toxic masochism was at least semi-contained.[11] Alas, while mentions of chakras and astrological transits are considered uncouth, it's weirdly socially acceptable to distasterbate in public, thus spreading our icky fear vibes far and wide, effectively smearing the whole darned planet in the stuff.

> *No form of thinking can take away the fear because the fear*
> *is there precisely because of the thinking.*
>
> **– Richard Rudd**

The thing is, change doesn't come from fear. Change comes from life – from the unbridled inspiration for better, brighter and more wonderful. Droning on and on about the perfect storm of apocalyptic X factors in which we are currently a-swirl activates those fear frequencies in our consciousness, as well as in everyone's within earshot, creating a slew of

---

11   Though, given that fear and suffering blow; plus, we're all connected, and that – on some dimension - you're anxiety is mine; and also, that I love you, I'd really prefer you not disasterbate at all, even in the private confines of your very own mind.

vibrational attractors, and essentially daring the universe to manifest these big, fat sucky visions, to say nothing of the nervous system toll all those fear hormones inevitably take on the body.

Alas, can we not with the apocalyptic bummer speak?

un, non, dis + less = ugh.

Allow me to point our attention towards the preface, wherein I introduced us to the word *omniscopic*. *Omniscopic* was created as a handy-dandy alternative to the words *limitless* and *unlimited*, which tether us to the frequency of *limitation*, given that it's impossible to speak either without also uttering the very "limit" they profess *not* to espouse.

With this in mind, I say fuck the *uns* and the *nons*. Fuck the prefixes and the suffixes that sidle up to low-vibe words, pretending to be a magical antidote to the downer frequencies they demand we utter. Why be *un-afraid*, when we can simply be *brave*? Why be *nonambiguous* when we can just be *clear*? Fuck *flawless*; how 'bout *perfect*[12]?

---

12   whatever that means

In Conclusion, Let Us Not with the Negative Space Speak.

The way we change our world for the infinitely more functional, sustainable, peaceful and rad is to speak from and into these very vibrational frequencies. It means brainstorming, discoursing and inviting others to share their visions of solutions, and best-case scenarios. It means dialoguing about what these new paradigm structures look like, and how they function, and what positive action steps we are to take to manifest a next-level global culture of abundant awesomeness. We change our world by speaking the vibratory upgrades we are calling in - continuously and persistently, emboldened by the assurance of their here and now *is*-ness.

Plus, it's way more fun than talking about all the sucky stuff. Just sayin'...

Quantum Langauging hack for *Negative Space Speak:*

Talk about what *is*, what you love, what you dream of, what inspires you, where you are going and what you are calling in. Praise, compliment, well-wish, thank. Speak gratitude; speak peace; speak awe; speak wonder; speak love.

Wash, rinse, repeat.

Declaring Challenges

Writing is hard, whines Would-Be Novelist X.

Of course it is, as it will continue to be, when we take it upon ourselves to declare that our chosen craft is "hard." And this isn't to say the act of putting words to paper/screen doesn't have its challenges, but to claim that it's "hard" is only to make it extra very much so, because – as we've already established – the universe is extremely obedient, and gives us exactly what we ask for, and then some.

When we take it upon ourselves to strap an endeavor with the "hard" label, we are, in fact, making it harder. Labeling our challenges obliterates the possibility of having an objectively neutral experience, instead filtering it through a predetermined story that does little (okay, nothing) to lighten our loads.

Quantum Languaging hacks for *hard*:

1. *Challenging* is an almost decent Quantum Langauging hack, as it implies a learning process, as well as a stretching of one's capabilities. Still, seeding *challenge* is a bold and risky move best left to martyrs, masochists and extreme athletes.

2. *Stimulating* is a fun hack, because it adds a visceral component to the situation. Except, it's a little vague, and has a tendency to get lost in translation. Use at your discretion.

3. My preference is to language challenges in the past, thus distancing myself from the adjective's frequencies, as in: *Whereas writing used to be challenging, I'm finding it gets easier and easier every time I do it.*

Granted, it's a little long-winded, and to this end, I encourage you to play around with your own load-lightning hacks. The key, really, is to language life, and the various steps that comprise it, as a dynamic process that is always in flux, such that we aren't tethered to any one experience of it. Impermanence rocks, and what was *hard* yesterday can absolutely be *easy* tomorrow, and is infinitely more likely to be so when we employ flexible languaging that isn't identified with potential challenges.

4. Rewrite the story about the task at hand for the easier and infinitely more fun, as in: *Writing is easy. This book is writing itself.*

Like *and Other Extraneous Space-Fillers*

Like slipped its wishy-washy way into West Coast vernacular in the power-packed 80s, a time of conservative right-wing rule tinged by Watergate memories, and shoulder pads. This otherwise useless *like* was embraced by Southern California teenagers with a collective yen for shopping, Bananarama and neon jumpsuits, and quickly spread like a linguistic virus across the planet, absolving its' utterers of any and all onus for the ideas that trailed its compulsive peppering.

The curse of *like* employed, not as reference to preference, rather as habitual modification of the allegation it precedes, is that it infuses those aforementioned words and concepts that trail it with an implied and thoroughly non-committal *out*.

Take, for example, Eduardo, who describes his friend's pet in saying: *It was, like, the smallest elephant in the world.*

In this instance, *like* frees Eduardo from any actual responsibility for what he is purporting to be true, such that the subject of his sentence may actually be a perfectly average-sized elephant, or a moth, or even a toenail.

The declarative: *He's the fastest runner in the state* becomes comparison, conjecture or hypothesis when phrased as: *He's, like, the fastest runner in the state;* which is to say he may be the fastest runner in the state, or he might just be similar to the fastest runner in the state – maybe in speed, possibly in his yen for Lycra hot pants. Who knows?

Beyond its unreliability as a useless modifier, *like*, along with its siblings *kind of, sort of,* and *ya' know,* has become an ubiquitous space-filler, an unconscious tic of tongue, and a whopping linguistic check-out – speckling the spaces between our words for no reason whatsoever, except to clue us into the fact that the speaker is not all that present, and is leaning on *like* just as a toddler clings to her favorite binky.

Quantum Languaging hack for *like*:

Get present.

Calling *Out* vs. Calling *In*

Folks on the spiritual path, humans who are "working" on themselves – we are the ones who "call each other *out.*" We do it when we witness a lapse in integrity, or a schism between action and intention, or when we are on the receiving end of a wayward *if,* or a careless *should.* It's a loving act – taking the time and energy to interrupt the conversational flow, and redirect the speaker's attention towards a shadow or a blind spot in service to their evolution. And yet, the phrase, *I'm calling you out,* does the action an energetic disservice.

The act of calling one *out* activates the frequency of the outcast archetype, which is deeply embedded in our DNA. Calling someone *out* triggers a deep, collective, primal wound, while implying ejection from the communal structure, which is traumatic on many levels.

No need stir up an ancient ouchie when we can simply call each other "in," thus inviting one another *into* deeper levels of self-inquiry/knowledge, as well as into the community weave.

Now, doesn't that feel better?

Separation Speak

Questioner: *How are we to treat others?*
Ramana Maharshi: *There are no others.*

Separation speak refers to any and all communication patterns that allege separation between ourselves and our fellow humans. It's the ego's favorite ruse – to pretend that we are somehow better, worse or qualitatively different than anyone else. It's also bullshit, because the real-deal, scientific truth of the matter is that we are a singular species, inextricably bound by DNA, self-reflective thought and a unified field of consciousness, not to mention the highs, lows, suffering and impermanence that every incarnate human experiences.

As a communication strategy, separation speak is super reckless in that it allows us to disassociate from our fellow humans, and to inflict any number of indignities and atrocities upon one another, because separation speak allows us to fool ourselves into thinking that there is an *us*, and that there is a *them*. Silly humans.

> *Our individuality, as people and as a species, is an illusion of bad language.*
>
> **– Terence McKenna**

There are myriad ways separation speak ekes its way into our communique, wreaking unchecked havoc on reputations, relationships, peace and sanity the world over. Let's break 'em down, shall we?

Name-calling, Ill-Willing, Hate-Speaking

Stapling a fixed identity to anyone based on a behavior pattern – regardless of how icky said behavior pattern is - is reductive, disassociative and super old p. It doesn't matter whether we call someone who hates a *hater,* or someone who hurts a *hurter,* name-calling means we are vibing low and contentious, making effective, compassionate communication (read: peaceful (r)evolutionizing) virtually impossible.

Name-calling triggers the objects of our ill-willing to shut way down, sending a flood of fear hormones into the brain and bloodstream, as a slew of psychological/emotional defense mechanisms come rushing in to protect. Duly contracted, these folks are now deaf to any salient points we might be offering along with our oh-so-clever insults. Again, it matters not a single lick whether we are directing our character assassinations toward those belonging to a formally marginalized minority group laying claim to the term *hate speech*, or whether we are attacking a member of the ruling elite; the emotional, psychological, physiological and energetic effects are one and the same in shutting folks way down, thus rendering collaborative problem-solving an incaccessible impossibility.

> *Don't be in such a hurry to condemn a person because he doesn't do what you do, or think as you think. There was a time when you didn't know what you know today.*
>
> **— Malcolm X**

Just because someone votes differently, lives differently, loves differently or worships differently than we do doesn't make them wrong, or bad, or the scapegoat for our every (or, even any) global atrocity; and calling them *bad* or *wrong* or *the every/any global atrocity scapegoat* isn't gonna get them to vote, live, love or worship the way we want them to; it's just gonna make them feel super unsafe, thus provoking them to cling even harder to the very points of view with which we are taking issue, while rendering our otherwise brilliant perspectives thoroughly inaudible.

The truth is that humans are infinitely more dynamic and complex than derisive behavior-based descriptives imply. And while the names we call others do nothing to promote peace, compassion or mutual understanding, they do wonders for reductive box-shoving, and the dehumanizing marginalization their careless bandying fosters. And whether our labels are accurate or deserved is an irrelevant dithering while Rome burns[13], because the fix for our current state of planetary wonkiness is wholly dependent upon our ability to evolve out of this tired old *right/wrong* paradigm, and to instead forge compassionate conversations that allow all parties to be heard and acknowledged while honing in on creative solutions that cultivate peace and unity for us all.

---

13   Reference appropriated from visionary genius, Terence McKenna, who said this:
"The artist's task is to save the soul of mankind; and anything less is a dithering while Rome burns. Because if the artists - who are self-selected for being able to journey into the Other - if the artists cannot find the way, then the way cannot be found."

Gossip

> *Gossip: a weed watered by wayward words.*

- Soul Dancer

Gossip is a thoroughly caustic, annoyingly ubiquitous cultural pastime wherein folks with a yen for distraction, and nothing better to do, take it upon themselves to talk about those who aren't present to weigh in on the topic at hand. It might not be all that terrible if we who were doing the gossiping were paragons of objective neutrality, sharing well-wishes and wonder, while reporting uneditorialized facts, precisely as they happened. Alas, we humans are not an objective lot. Filtered through our individual wounds and perspectives, stories get skewed, opinions get passed off as fact, and Truth gets mangled by unchecked judgments, which – in turn - shape other people's associations. Gossip destroys reputations and relationships, while eroding trust and community, and tarnishing our collective field with misinformation, distorted opinions and icky, sticky vibes.

It would be one thing if the brain gave equal credence to both bad-mouthing and acclaim. Alas, our complex neural mechanisms seem to have a perverse yen for the negative, which means that for every five wonderful descriptives we offer about someone, the brain will cling to that one[14] bitchy, backstabby comment we uttered back when Mercury

---

14   Numbers are approximations. Not all numbers, obviously, just the ones in this sentence.

was retrograde, and we were triggered, and took it upon ourselves to slander Sentient Being X, or relay a lopsided version of Uncomfortable Situation Q.

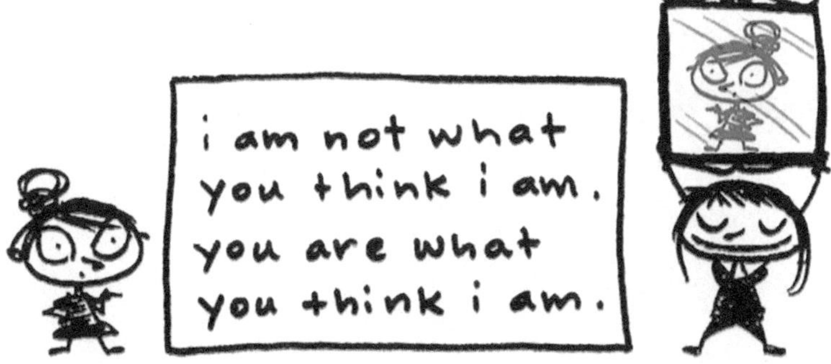

The reality is that any charge we have on someone else's behavior is only ever a reflection of our own unresolved shadows, which means that when we are struck with the urge to speak negatively about folks, our wisest move is to turn that critical lens inward, and milk the itch for all the super, über valuable illuminations it holds about ourselves.

Quantum Languaging hacks for *separation speak*:

Hacking the separation speak situation really comes down to the Buddhist precept of *Right Speech*, which prescribes three[15] simple communication

---

15   Okay, four: *Don't curse.* Except, fuck that.

tenets that – when consistently employed - attune our frequencies to the highest good for all beings:

1. *Speak truth.*

    Do not lie. Do not mislead. Do not withhold.

2. *Speak kindness.*

    Speak no ill-will.

3. *Speak wholeness.*

    Do not gossip.

PART 4

Communication Tools to Add to the Arsenal

Present Moment Languaging

Time is not the stable moving staircase that prosemen have for centuries pretended it to be, but an unaccountable wibble-wobble.

— Robert Graves

We are programmed to think of time as a sort of linear conveyor belt, inching us forward from point a. (birth) to point b. (death) – with a handful of noteworthy stops along the way. The fundamental problem with this scenario is that time is a fourth dimensional construct that exists omnidirectionally and simultaneously, on multiple dimensions at once, which is to say that time isn't at all linear, and that past and future are make-believe conceptual abstractions that don't even exist.

There's no need to strain your brain trying to grok this, as the human mind is - as yet - shaped by/confined to third-dimensional reality, which necessarily distorts our relationship to time. What is relevant, however, is that the present moment is really, truly all there is, which makes for a powerful reality creation precept, as well as the key to peaceful (r)evolution/life itself. To this end, when referencing our goals, dreams and destiny, present moment languaging is our BFF.

It's why I don't say: *I am going to write a New York Times Best Seller*, or: *I hope my book will make the Best Seller list*. I say: *I am writing a New York Times Best Seller*. Feel the difference?

In languaging our intentions in the present, we collapse any perceived distance between ourselves and our highest visions, and declare them in the here and now. At the same time, we adjust our internal frequencies to match the vibration of our manifest visions, while claiming the authority to name their presence and their successful *is*-ness...now.

Powerful, right?

Past-Tense the Shadows.

This moment - right here, right now - is brand, spankin' new. It never was before, nor will it ever be again. Think of all the factors at play: you – a complex, ever-shifting collection of atoms, cells, bone, blood, thoughts, hopes, dreams, desires, fears and shadows, balancing on a living, breathing, spinning rock, which is itself orbiting a pulsing star while hurtling through previously uncharted realms of deeper and deeper space. None of us have ever been here before, nor will we ever be again. This moment is totally new, as are these precise iterations of you, and of me. As sovereign, dynamic beings, we can absolutely liberate ourselves from the shadows of our past by making a different choice **now**.

This is why when referencing challenges, limiting beliefs, disempowering habits, et al, we attune ourselves to the frequency of our sovereignty by framing our experiences in the past, which cleans our vibrational slate, and frees us up to embody upgraded versions **now**.

Example:

Historically, I have been challenged to commit to a monogamous relationship for an extended period of time.

Jeremy is 42. His longest relationship lasted four months, and three of them were long distance. But, Jeremy is shifting; and Jeremy is doing his work – looking at his dissociative tendencies, as well as his mommy issues; and really committing to opening his heart. As such, Jeremy can speak honestly about his relationship history while not shackling himself to an outdated behavior pattern, or the energetics that informed it.

Past-tensing our shadows is a super effective langauging hack that allows us to communicate openly and honestly about issues and challenges without having to identify ourselves with them, or invoke their frequencies in the present moment.

"Clear, Cancel, Delete."

Mastering a language of deliberate intent takes practice. For as many years as we've been alive, we've amassed a comparable collection of unconscious communication patterns that infuse our every exchange. To choose to shift them for the more efficient, effective and expansive takes courage, commitment and compassion, as we will likely make mistakes along the way. While it is not my intention to project any unconscious slips of tongue or keyboard upon you, it is my experience – several years into my own Quantum Languaging practice – that habits take time to unravel.

Clear, cancel, delete is a nifty little Quantum Languaging hack that allows us to shift any vibrational wonkiness our habitual utterings may inspire, while freeing us up to re-language the statements in a more empowering fashion. Sure, it used to feel a little weird interrupting myself mid-sentence to utter a supremely nerdy-sounding string of words, and then immedi-ately re-language my statement in service to vibrational harmony, but feeling weird is pretty much par for the transformational path. Initially. Because the truth is, it's not "me" who feels weird, it's my ego, indulging in a dash of self-reflective vanity, and second-guessing how I'm coming off to others. The good news is that this sort of self-consciousness is a temporary phase we pass through en route to autonomous confidence, and the well-earned luxury of not giving a single shit what others may or may not think of us, because we know who we are, and we love ourselves unconditionally, and we have way bigger fish to fry.

Ask for Definitions.

How often do we find ourselves in an argument, only to realize - at the tail end, emotions raging, pulses soaring, heart beats thumping - that we weren't actually talking about the same thing? We assumed we knew what the other person was talking about because, on some level, we know what the words they were using mean. Still, for every word we use, there exists a multitude of definitions, as well as an infinite variety of nuance, assumption and association overlaid atop its official connotation(s), which are then garnished with our own personal filters and projections. All this is to say, shared definitions are extremely rare.

"I'm not feeling dharmically inclined to go to your performance tonight," Fred tells his wife, Emma, mere minutes before she is scheduled to leave for the theater.

"But, you said—wait," she pauses, breathing deep into her lower belly while counting to three. "What do you mean by 'dharmically inclined'?"

The question allows Fred to explain his sudden burst of inspiration, and his inclination to stay home, and dive into his creative process, while supporting Emma in understanding where Fred is coming from, such that she can wish him a productive session before heading off to dazzle yet another audience with her genius. See how easy relationships can be? ;)

Asking folks to define their terms doesn't just engender intellectual clarity and relational harmony, it begets intimacy, inviting us to dig deeper into our own processes, and to share from those depths. Besides, it's generally only our egos that keep us from asking *What do you mean by that?* or *How are you defining _____ in this context?* because said egos grow bigger and stronger by being omniscient and right. When we invite clarification, we run the risk of lending the impression that we don't know absolutely all there is about every little thing. So what?

The Little *Nos* that Serve the Bigger *YES*

So often, we opt out of saying *No* because we are afraid of hurting someone else's feelings; of coming off as rude or insensitive; or of burning a bridge, or shutting a door. The thing is, *No* is a super valuable tool when it comes to transforming our reality for the better, because staying focused on the new paradigm we are stewarding demands vigilence and discernment. And so we offer compassionate *nos* to the activities that invite focus, energy and resources we simply don't have the bandwidth to share; and, in this way, the little *nos* pave the pathway to our biggest *yeses*.

To opt out of articulating an authentic *No* for fear of hurting someone else's feelings is arrogant, codependent and super, very twisted. It is not on us to micromanage anyone else's emotions, nor to bend the truth in service to our very limited ideas as to what might be best for someone else's process. When we withhold the truth for fear of hurting another, we second-guess their maturity, their autonomy and their capacity for wholeness, while denying them the opportunity to flex their emotional intelligence muscles. Condescending, much? The beauty of the well-placed, compassionate *no* is that is allows us the chance to foster emotional strength, and stamina, while availing ourselves to the genuine opportunities waiting on the flip side of our honest *nos*.

91

Quantum Languaging Practice:

Practice saying "No" without concern for how you are being received, or how personally the receiver may, or may not, be taking it. Be honest. Be authentic. Be compassionate. Watch what comes up for you when you say the word: "No." Work with the sensations. Allow all of it to surface so that you can see what's there, and then dig deeper to uncover the thought forms that are informing the feelings. Be patient. Be kind. Be curious.

Part 5:

Quantum Languaging Concepts to Consider

Thoughts Totally Count.

This Quantum Languaging (r)evolution extends light years beyond the words we use to communicate with others, to include the ones we silently direct towards ourselves. *Hello, self-talk!* You know, those ever-looping commentaries whispered in the cavernous confines of our minds? The ones that accompany us throughout our every waking moment? Yeah, those. Scientists who study this sort of thing estimate we cycle through about 20-60,000 "thoughts" per day. The thing is, this running commentary is by no means an original collection of *a-has*, rather a largely recycled batch of habitual thoughts and judgments that weave themselves together to form our belief systems.

Be mindful of your self-talk, it's a conversation with the universe.

— David James Lee

Our beliefs are hardwired into our neurology through repetition. Duly programmed, our brains process and interpret incoming data based on these beliefs. In this way, beliefs not only serve as filtering frameworks for our perception of reality, they shape it at a fundamental level.

With this in mind, let us consider our self-talk patterns, along with our interpersonal communication habits, as we employ these Quantum Languaging hacks. I speak from experience when I say that, while this material has done wonders in supporting my communication prowess with others, the most transformative application has come from applying it to my self-talk. And while the process of unraveling the beliefs and the thought forms informing our behavior can indeed be confronting, as well as humbling, it's well worth it for the chance to rewrite them all for the infinitely more supportive – a thoroughly empowering task that happens to also be super, very fun.

Example:

Sadie was going through a rough patch – navigating a dark and shadowy spell marked by the belief that nobody cared about her. While feeling alone in every sense of the word, as well as supremely sorry for herself, Sadie became aware of a consistent thought ringing through her head at least several dozen times a day: *I don't care.*

She'd hear about a party she wasn't invited to.
I don't care, Sadie would think.

A(nother) publisher rejected her manuscript.
I don't care, Sadie said to herself.

Her latest crush didn't text her back.
I don't care, she muttered into her lonely abyss.

The thing is, if Sadie herself was claiming not to care, then why would the Universe offer her experiences of care? The more Sadie watched her thoughts, the more she realized she was pushing away the very thing she wanted by denying it over and over and over again. Because, as we've already established, the subconscious mind takes repetitive thoughts like *I don't care* super, very literally, and thus goes about shaping and filtering reality to match our requests. In saying *I don't care,* Sadie was literally programming her reality to be devoid of care.

> *But if thought corrupts language, language can also corrupt thought.*
>
> **– George Orwell**

And so it was that Sadie took to hacking this thought for an infinitely more preferable experience. To this day, when Sadie catches herself thinking *I don't care,* she *clears,* she *cancels,* she *deletes,* and then she restates the idea for the infinitely more supportive: *I care; and I am cared for,* thus rewiring her brain, and rewriting her reality in the process. Yay.

Quantum Languaging Practice:

Allow yourself 15-20 minutes in a quiet, comfortable space. Write down all the negative thoughts you have about yourself - the big ones (*I'm not smart enough; I'm a failure; I'm ugly*) and the little ones (*I can't play air hockey; My feet are gross; I hate my laugh*) - leaving at least one line of space between each one. Be thorough.

After you've completed your list, go back through it, starting at the top, rewriting each statement such that it is positive and supportive. Be brave. Be creative. Be compassionate. Most of all, have fun.

A sampling of Quantum Self-Talk hacks:

I'm not smart enough.
I am a highly intelligent person.
I am committed to learning about __________ and to increasing
my competency in _____________________.

I'm a failure.
I am success personified.
I vibrate at the frequency of success.
I am ready for success.
I deserve success.

I'm ugly.
I am beautiful.
I adhere to a higher standard of beauty that allows me to
know my gorgeousness from the inside out.

I can't play air hockey.
I get better at air hockey every time I play.
It's fun to see myself improving so consistently.
I am committed to improving my air hockey game.
I enjoy playing air hockey my own unique way.

I have weird feet.
I love my feet.
I am grateful for healthy, functional feet.
I appreciate my spunky little appendages for supporting me,
and moving me forward in my life so consistently and so well.

Make use of this practice whenever you catch yourself thinking (or articulating) a negative thought about yourself, immediately reframing the statement for the positive. Be diligent, regardless of how silly it sounds. Keep reframing. Keep restating. Know that you are rewiring your brain, and rewriting your reality in the process.

Baby Steps Rock.

Let us note that every word matters, even the low-vibing ones. When utilized mindfully, our unconscious communication patterns, as well as our negative self-talk, can actually be useful tools that illuminate the limiting belief systems holding us back. It takes courage to look our shadows in the eye, and to see our patterns for what they truly are. It is also our redemption. As such, I encourage us to arm ourselves with tremendous wellsprings of kindness, compassion and equanimity, and to spend some time considering our negative thoughts and beliefs, and, ultimately, to observe how they are shaping our lives. With this in mind, we may find it helpful, initially, to move slowly with our Quantum Languaging hacks and revisions, so that we can see where we contract around our efforts to expand. I find that when I hone in on a previously undiscovered negative belief, it can sometimes feel awkward or cringey to articulate the upgrade, because the higher-vibing iteration isn't yet aligned with the beliefs that have historically held me back. This is where baby steps come in. For instance, it might not (yet) be appropriate to leap from the distorted belief that *I don't deserve love*, to *I am high-vibing, heart-centered partnership*. And that's perfectly okay. There are plenty of other empowering options that will allow me to shift my thoughts, my beliefs and my frequency as I transmute the wounds and traumas that inspired the disempowering thought in the first place. So, *I am willing to open myself to love*, and *I am committed to knowing myself as lovable and deserving of partnership.* These interim upgrades allow me to authentically honor my process while I raise my vibration and expand into higher and more expansive expressions of my Self.

Quantum Self-Talk Checklist:

When examining our self-talk, we are wise to ask ourselves the following questions, and to be diligent in aligning our internal monologues with a slew of *Yeses:*

Is it kind?

Is it compassionate?

Is it true?

Is it serving me?

Is it in alignment with my goals, my dreams, my dharma and my destiny?

Is it something I would feel comfortable and aligned saying to a small child?

The More the Merriest

There's no getting around it; mastering these Quantum Languaging hacks takes practice. While the concepts are simple, the process of shifting our habituated communication patterns is no small feat. No man is an island; and that whole interdependent thing our species is rocking gets really relevant when it comes to hacking our languaging patterns for the better. They don't call 'em "blind spots" for nothing. I won't go so far as to say it's *impossible* to consciously attune to our every word in every moment by ourselves (because *impossible* is a limiting belief, and free will rocks), but, it's a heck of a lot easier to track habitual old p. languaging patterns when we have community to help point our attention towards them in real time.

To this end, I recommend sharing these Quantum Languaging hacks far and wide, while rallying a willing and enthusiastic herd of Quantum Languaging comrades with whom we can trade loving languaging reflections in service to our respective and collective mastery, as well as peaceful (r)evolution, and an abundant, thriving, unified planet Earth.

Ask Permission.

Be sure to get permission before offering a Quantum Languaging hack, regardless of how close you may be to the speaker. Without a pre-established agreement to trade tough truths and reflections, the well-intentioned act of calling someone in on their communication patterns can backfire. Avoid potential drama/ego-ruffling by making sure to ask permission before offering reflections and hacks.

Quantum Languaging Permission-Asking options:

Are you open to a reflection?
May I share what I see?
Are you interested in hearing another perspective?
Are you available to receive a Quantum Languaging hack?

Mastery, Mindfulness and Practice, Oh My!

The beauty of these languaging hacks is that their application requires no techy apps, no membership fees and no moisture-wicking performance apparel. We use words all day, every day; and given that it takes approximately 10,000 hours of practice to master *anything*, the likelihood of rocking a next-level Quantum Languaging practice/paradigm in our lifetime is extraordinarily high. Once we know the hacks, mastery is merely a matter of practice. As such, language becomes our sadhana[16] - a moment-to-moment presence practice that invites mindfulness and discernment, while rewarding our efforts with an upleveled reality that meets and surpasses our loveliest imaginings for the greatest good of all.

Your mission, should you choose to accept it, is to incorporate these Quantum Languaging hacks into your moment-to-moment meanderings - to pause between words, to feel into vibrational frequencies, to speak peace and unity and omniscopic possibility into our unified field, while stewarding this great, grand, paradigm-shattering shift into a higher and more expansive expression of consciousness and culture and community in service to all Life, while having the best time ever (yet).

---

16   **sadhana**; *n.* a spiritual practice or discipline that leads to perfection